# Strictly Business

*How to Crush it as a Young Entrepreneur*

**Brendan Cox**
**With Lauren Kamienski**

Brendan Cox

To my parents and sister who have supported me non-stop through my numerous business ventures. My family has been there for me every step of the way and without them I wouldn't have accomplished anything.

# Table of Contents:

# Introduction

## Hi. My name is Brendan.

If you're reading this, I'm assuming it's for one of these reasons:

1. **You're an aspiring entrepreneur** and you know who I am. Maybe you're familiar with a few of my past businesses, or you follow me on one of my social media platforms. If so, thanks for supporting me on this journey. I hope you're ready to learn the side of me I haven't fully shared.

2. **You're unsure of what to do next** and you need my help. Lucky for you, what you're about to read is a raw and honest reflection of the things I learned on my journey to becoming one of the most successful entrepreneurs at my age. Hopefully my story motivates you to do whatever it is you've been wanting to do.

3. **You found this by chance** and now you're curious. You might be a businessperson, you might not. Either way, it's nice to meet you. I hope something in here resonates with you.

No matter the reason you're here, I'm happy to have you. I've been wanting to share my business journey for a while, but I've been busy keeping my head in the game. I'm still grinding (I always am), but I'm finally ready to share everything - stories, tips, secrets, tricks - about how I got here.

The truth is, I myself am still trying to understand what's important in the business world. I don't think I'll ever have it perfect - I don't think anyone will. Education should always be a lifelong process. But I want to share with you all what I know to be true and the lessons I've learned, through my own personal experiences.

You might be wondering who I am to be giving business advice. You might be asking "Who would take advice from a 20-year-old?" "Who is this kid?" **And I'll tell you.**

I was a kid who was driven for success, and now I am a successful young adult. And I didn't get here with anything special - no extra money, no famous family, no freebies. My progress was driven solely by pure, undying motivation, and the ability to learn from absolutely everything I do. Anyone can get to where I am today - it's simple. **You just have to want it.**

# Who Am I?

I'm Brendan Cox and I'm 20. This all feels really official, but I'm just an average kid from a suburb in Central Jersey. There's nothing particularly special about me. I grew up in a nice house, in a nice, quiet town and I had a regular childhood full of friends, family, and fun. I went to school, played sports, and did all those normal kid things. But there was always something a little different about me.

I grew up with my older sister who I always looked up to, and my incredibly dedicated and loving parents who gave us both a comfortable childhood. My dad works for a major book publishing company and my mom is a pretty awesome interior designer. Their motivation has always driven me, and they have always taught me the importance of working hard for what you want.

Truthfully, I wouldn't be here without the things they have given me, and I can never thank them enough for the love and support they have shown me. When I picture who I want to be someday, it looks just like both of them. They have provided me with everything I have ever needed, which is what drove me to want to be able to provide for myself.

As a kid, I often found myself wanting things I didn't need, and I didn't see any reason to burden my parents' wallets with continued silly requests. Instead, I wanted to make my own money to be able to buy things on my own (I still didn't *need* that stuff, but you get the point).

My sister and other girls I knew didn't seem to have this problem because they could babysit. They could walk next door and ask the neighbor if they needed a sitter, and that was a quick 50 bucks which could easily be repeated. For me it was different. I was a little boy. Who would trust a boy, let alone a young one, with a kid? (Not that I wanted to take care of kids anyway. No thanks.) It seemed unfair to me that my money-making options were so limited at my age. How could I earn the spending money I wanted?

I was always fascinated by the idea of business and how simple it was to provide products or services for money. If you think about it, business exists everywhere - your Netflix account, your morning coffee, your daily commute, even the paper you're reading this on. Our modern world is a series of transactions between companies and consumers, products and buyers, services and clients. Every single thing is supplied, demanded, and paid for. Is that not freaking crazy?

Well, little me thought so. From a young age (I'm talking like, 7 years old), I was a hustler. I remember begging my mom to let me set up a lemonade stand outside the house so I could make a couple bucks. A few dollars here and a few dollars there. It was nothing crazy, but it was exhilarating. And it was never the actual money that fascinated me - it was the idea that I was providing a service that people actually wanted. It was a passion that burned inside of me. A need for business that combusted into a yearning for success.

So I decided I needed to start a business of my own - something unique to my talents that also made me money. I was only a little kid, so my span of skills wasn't that expansive yet. I had to think of something easy enough that I could be successful in (I mean, I wasn't a prodigy or anything), and I had to pick something affordable enough to be worth it.

One thing I liked a lot at that age was music. I spent a lot of time on YouTube watching music videos and videos about mixing songs. It became something I was really interested in, and I gradually taught myself the basics of how to mix music. I essentially was a self-taught DJ, which was something unique and just interesting enough that I thought it could surely make me some cash. So, that Christmas, I asked for DJ equipment and, to my surprise, I received it, with all the bells and whistles (still can't thank Santa enough for coming in so clutch).

Beginning that morning, I was determined to create a successful DJ business for locals to use and enjoy. Not only did I want to make money, but I was also genuinely driven to make people happy. (That's one of the most important things I can tell you - you need to enjoy making people happy. Seriously. There's nothing more rewarding.)

I started with volunteering at local events that needed entertainment but couldn't pay. I DJed at multiple school events and town gatherings for free, which eventually led to the spread of my business. Parents and kids who had attended my events took my information and either hired me themselves or referenced my service to others. Word of mouth was the reason my business succeeded (because this was *just* before the whole Facebook-mom era. Hmm .. blessing or curse?). Before I knew it I was DJing at countless school events, community engagement nights, birthday bashes, block parties, and bar-mitzvahs.

I kept the DJ thing going for a while and it made me a good amount of money. I'm not talking six figures, but it was a lot for little Brendan, and it definitely allowed me more flexibility in buying the things I wanted. It was also a genuine fun time - I was working but I was also doing something I enjoyed. The business was successful for a few years, but when I was about 13 it stopped being fun for me. Over time, I naturally lost interest in it - it just wasn't the same as when I started, and I lost touch with it. RIP. (To my DJ equipment, if you're reading this, I want you to know it wasn't your fault.)

When I put down my headphones for the last time, I knew I would need something to replace the business I would be losing. Like I said, it wasn't about the money. I had made enough money DJing to continue on as an unemployed middle schooler, but I still wanted something to keep me busy. I was still as driven as ever to be successful. I needed something to satisfy my hunger for business.

I remember being in sixth grade and staying up until 2 or 3 in the morning just scouring the internet for different ways I could possibly make money. I would sit for hours and think about my options. I went over countless business models and obviously had a few other ideas I had to rule out before I landed on what would end up being my next and arguably most important endeavor to date: Kicks Cases.

The idea for the business came from a trend I had always noticed throughout my young life: people loved to represent their favorite athletes. Whether it was through clothes, shoes, hats, stickers, or wall decals (everyone had a Fathead. Let's be honest), almost everyone I knew had some way of showing the world who their favorite player was. I began brainstorming ways I could make this work, but in a unique way that hadn't been done before - I couldn't just stick an athlete on a shirt and call it a day. It was going to take more than that.

So, I built upon another trend I was noticing - phone cases. Everyone (and I mean EVERYONE) was obsessed with phone cases when I was in middle school - the fancy bedazzled ones, the ones with quotes on them, the furry ones, even the ones that made your whole phone look like an animal (these were some scary times). I thought for sure that if I sold phone cases, my business would be at the top, and the idea was perfect. Not only would I put the sports player on the phone case, but the player would also be dunking, catching, or passing the Apple logo as if it was a ball. Most of the kids I knew already had iPhones, and what does almost everyone have on their iPhone? Yup, a case. It would be the perfect company to attract customers of all ages. It was genius.

I guess that's where my first little business spiel comes in - **if you're going to start a company, you need to be offering a product or service that, for the most part, everyone NEEDS.** You're not going to get any business if your product is less than necessary. (And when I say necessary, I don't mean like, food and water. I mean something that someone is going to see and think, "Holy crap I need that!" even if it's stupid. You know how people are. I mean, there's a company that delivers elephant poop to your door. If it's interesting enough, people will want it, even if they don't *need* it.)

My phone case design was simple yet incredibly intriguing - it was transparent with an athlete of the customer's choice on it, and that athlete would be playing his/her sport with the Apple logo as the ball. After drawing out the concept on paper, I purchased Adobe Photoshop and began working with my designs. I watched countless informational videos on how to cut out images and place them onto phone cases. The idea became more and more intriguing and extremely easy to execute. I learned a lot throughout the process (at least more than I was expected to be learning at that age).

Through a very popular wholesale supplier website called Alibaba, I was able to connect with a manufacturer in Shenzhen, China who would be able to help me with production. He didn't know I was only in middle school (to be fair, he never asked!), but he was interested in pursuing the business with me, so we decided to partner up. (I still wonder what would have happened if he found out I was only 13. He probably would have laughed and deleted the email.)

From then on, he was essentially my business partner - I'd send him my design mockups and he would do the leg work. This involved creating the case molds in a factory and making sure the player lined up perfectly with the logo. He then would send me the cases and I would ship them out from my home. This process continued the whole time the company existed.

I remember sitting in class all day and waiting for the last bell to ring so I could get home to either make more designs or open the boxes of cases that were shipped to me daily. During the day, I would also be itching to pull out my phone and connect with my followers. I had created a whole new life outside of school that my peers couldn't understand. I was a businessman now.

Kicks Cases was only able to succeed through the power of social media, and this is where my next biggest tip comes in: **your business needs a social media presence.** If Instagram and Facebook hadn't existed, neither would Kicks Cases. After our initial launch, our social media presence began to gradually blow up, eventually amassing over 111,000 followers across multiple platforms. Before I knew it, we had orders coming from every single state in America, and followers from all over the world.

And I know what you're thinking … How the heck did I get *that* many followers selling phone cases? Perhaps you've tried your luck in the past with Instagram followers. And you were probably disappointed, because it *is* very hard to grow a reliable and dedicated Instagram following. There are tips and tricks I'm still learning, but what I know for a fact is that **it's crucial. You need to have social**

**media.** Even if that means posting a picture to the same 3 followers every single day. Too many people make the mistake of giving up prematurely, before they have steady shareable content and valuable followers. No one ever told you that it was possible to blow up your Instagram in a week, and if they did, they were lying. It takes time and consistency to grow your following. If you stop working at it, you'll never get there. I know it sounds cliché, but you just have to keep going. Post, post, and post again. Reach out. Advertise. Develop relevant content. It's worth it - take it from 13-year-old me.

Kicks Cases didn't become successful in a day. I had to watch a lot of my posts crash and burn before I finally got to see my idea going viral through Facebook and Instagram. Eventually, with the help of targeted advertisements on social media platforms, we soon became one of the largest and most successful companies of our kind. We had thousands of customers across the country and shipped cases out every single day. Our social media platforms were huge and people loved our products. It was everything I had dreamed of and more.

Don't get me wrong - I was only 13, so it wasn't as easy as it sounds. I needed a lot of help from my parents. I didn't have a driver's license, so my mom had to help me with the logistics. She would take all of the packages to the post office every single day, eventually giving herself the title of Kicks Cases' "not-for-profit shipping clerk." (She deserved it, she basically lived at the post office.) On the other hand, my dad helped me with the professional side of things. He made sure my emails sounded like they were coming from an adult and did most of the talking during serious negotiations. (He was a pretty good bodyguard, too.)

After the first full year of Kicks Cases' opening, we were not only fulfilling thousands of online orders, but our products were in display cases in sneaker stores across New Jersey. My cases sat strategically at the check-out counter, and the idea was that consumers would purchase a phone case alongside an expensive pair of shoes. Sales skyrocketed. Every month, I would visit the stores to restock with new displays featuring our hottest products, and I would speak with the store owners about that month's sales.

Kicks Cases thrived as the top provider of these types of phone cases for about 3 years until copycat brands inevitably started to take over. I learned the hard way that **being at the top comes with competing entrepreneurs who are trying to make money off of your idea.** By the time my company reached its peak, there were 10-20 other brands marketing similar products. The athlete-phone-case industry exploded, and my idea was no longer original, despite being my own from the very beginning.

Until then, I didn't fully understand the importance of protecting my ideas. As a young CEO, I hadn't yet learned about patents, and therefore never obtained one to protect this idea. Even though Kicks Cases was still superior to the other brands because of our massive following and professional, consistent content, our business gradually fell off the map. By then, there were so many copycat brands, it would be impossible for me to ever receive credit for the trend I started. This was one of the biggest challenges I faced as a young entrepreneur - I had finally met the uglier side of the business world.

The fall of Kicks Cases can't be solely attributed to its competition - I had built a company off of a trend that would inevitably die, like all other trends do. **If a business is based on a trend, it will either evolve with that trend or cease to exist.** I didn't see the company evolving any further, as I was naturally starting to lose interest in it as well. It just wasn't realistic to keep the company going, so I decided to move on to my next venture. (No hard feelings, Kicks Cases.)

During my time selling those phone cases, I picked up various skills and tricks that helped me stay relevant on social media. Being a young entrepreneur, I had always been told that I should never have just one stream of income, so I was determined to continue making money on Instagram. My eyes had been opened up to the endless possibilities of social media.

With this determination and my past successes in mind, I was sure I would be able to succeed again on social media. I decided to buy an Instagram account with a following of over 200,000 people for $900. It was a big investment and definitely scared me, but it would soon prove to be worth it.

The account I purchased had a sports niche (can you tell I was an average teenage boy? Is it obvious?), which was both popular and lucrative at the time. I posted sponsored content daily which included shoutouts and advertisements for hundreds of smaller accounts looking to grow. Within the first week, I made my $900 back and then some. It all seemed so easy.

I got addicted to the "Instagram Game," which is the unofficial term for the business side of Instagram. This is essentially the word that refers to all of those advertisements you see - I was paid by countless companies to simply post their information on my account, and I made a significant amount of money this way. It's all just part of a game.

The directly paid ads were making me a good chunk of change, but I wanted to explore other ways I could monetize my following. The secrets of Instagram were tricky to uncover, but I eventually learned about pay-per-click companies, which essentially pair you with advertisers who are looking to inorganically attract traffic on their pages. So, I would post an ad, and each time the link received a "click," or the page being advertised was visited, I received money from the company I was advertising. Most of these advertisements came in the form of app downloads - I advertised an app, and if my followers clicked the link, I received money. I received even more money if they downloaded the app. (Important message from everyone currently advertising an app: Please download the app. Even if you delete it right away. Just please.)

I continued advertising for a while because it was a steady and reliable source of income that I greatly profited from. It was also something I had mastered along the way, so it became much easier for me to handle. I was only posting about 3 ads a day (which virtually required no effort), but I was making a lot of money. Upon realizing how profitable one Instagram account could be, I decided to open numerous other accounts through which I could advertise. Before I knew it, I had amassed a combined following of over 1 million unique people across my different accounts.

Not only did I know how to effectively advertise, but I now had multiple Instagram accounts I could advertise from, which led to what was the beginning of a successful Social Media Management business. Because I had so many platforms, and each of them was doing well, other companies looked to me for assistance. I partnered with large corporations including Crep Protect, Laced Up Laces, and Reshoevn8r, offering package deals that included advertisements across all of my accounts on a monthly basis. Offering these packages ended up being one of my best ideas, as I generated consistent income and was able to watch businesses succeed by connecting target audiences to advertisers eager to reach a large following.

While advertisements were the majority of my content, I needed to create consistent and eye-catching content for my loyal followers (shout-out to the real ones who still followed, even after I posted a thousand ads). I had gotten into graphic design with Kicks Cases, but I never had the chance to focus solely on design because I was always so busy with other ventures.

With my design experience and a bunch of followers under my belt, I started to create original content for my Instagram pages. This included information, promotions, quotes, tips, and just about anything else you can think of - I started to develop all of my content myself, and I even began making content for some of my larger clients. I created advertisements, flyers, brochures, sale pictures, and I even started making logos. I was fascinated by fonts, color palettes, and editing tricks I wouldn't have otherwise learned. It became a passion that I still have today.

It wasn't until someone reached out to me directly, without ever having heard of me, that I realized the value I had created. I had only ever done graphics for clients because I knew how to, because I could use Photoshop, because it was convenient - a quick buck. Little did I know, I would soon be doing graphics because people wanted my designs. **It stopped being about the fact that I knew how to do it and became about the fact that I was good at it.**

After spotting some of my designs, a Brooklyn-based clothing company reached out to me for graphic design help. They had seen my work with Kicks Cases and my content for other clients and were extremely interested in partnering with me. I designed their clothing line, but the company unfortunately went out of business due to the size of its niche - it mainly targeted people in Brooklyn and therefore lost any room for expansion. While this seemed like the end of my journey with this company, it was only the beginning.

In 2017, the owners of that company, brothers Eli and Spencer Zeid, launched a second line of clothing, dubbed Habits 365. Having loved my original designs so much, the brothers wanted me to partner with them once again. I was officially hired as the graphic designer for Habits 365, and I still work with them today. From the time that I started with them until now, the company has absolutely exploded. I've made thousands of designs for their line, some of which have been worn by renowned celebrities including Dwayne Wade, LeVeon Bell, and Russell Wilson. Countless rappers have also worn my designs, including Jay Critch, Da Baby, & A Boogie Wit Da Hoodie. My journey with this company has not only gotten me the recognition I deserve for my work, but it has also allowed me to make numerous helpful connections. The same way Eli and Spencer found me, other companies were able to find me through Habits 365 and ask about my graphic design services.

I decided it was time to give my services their own name so I could actually create a working business out of what I was doing. I called it Cox Visuals, based on my last name (original, I know), and I began branding this as if it was any other business. I created an account for Cox Visuals on multiple social media platforms including Instagram, Facebook, and Twitter, and I began marketing my services to make it easier for larger companies to find me. With Habits 365 as my first official customer, my client list began to grow and I eventually found myself creating designs for numerous well-known businesses.

Cox Visuals has been thriving since I made my very first design. I've done major work with some other really big companies, and I've learned so much from every project I've done. One of my favorite projects to date is the SocialStudy App - it's basically the Uber for tutors, and a genius idea overall. It started when two students from Emory University saw my graphics and reached out to me with their ideas for this app. I created various mockups, which are basically digital versions of what the app is supposed to look like - the functionalities of the app, the colors, the fonts, everything. Because there are hundreds of different screens that can possibly be shown on this app, I had to create a mockup for each individual page so the mockups took almost two years to finish and perfect. The app is currently in the process of being coded so it can be launched, and there are high hopes for its success.

Since the beginning of my graphic design business, I've partnered with so many different companies and expanded both my skill set and my credibility immensely. Cox Visuals was born from a genuine passion - it was never driven by money - and it's something I'm really proud of. Today, I am connecting with various large brands and influencers for graphic design work, and my designs are often featured on larger platforms which continue to attract new clients on a daily basis.

Even though I've always had my plate full with social media and graphic design, I wanted to keep working and thinking of new ideas. As a kid, I knew I was capable of achieving more and that same drive followed me throughout my life. I was always doing so much, but it never felt like enough - **I needed more.**

Throughout high school, I wasn't into the stuff everyone else was doing - I didn't go out to parties, I never drank or did drugs, and I was always 100% focused on my business ventures. A lot of people didn't understand me, and I lost touch with a lot of friends due to our different interests. My version of fun has always been work - I never wanted to do anything else. Because of this, I became known as the "entrepreneur kid," and many of my peers would contact me for business and money-making ideas. (I guess no one's interested in you until they hear you're making money.)

With my peers and my personal dedication in mind, I started thinking of ways I could make money while also providing my friends with jobs (you know, share the wealth). The summer after my sophomore year in high school, I was doing a lot of yard work for neighbors. Local adults would pay me to do simple tasks they didn't have time for, like mowing the lawn, pulling weeds, or moving furniture around. I realized how large the demand was for teenagers doing those annoying, everyone-has-to-do-it, I'll-do-it-next-week, household jobs. I talked to my parents, and they explained to me how things were during their childhood - kids would do jobs like this all the time for some extra cash, but these days, teens are nowhere to be found.

Ultimately, I made a business out of it (which I've learned you can pretty much do with anything). I called it "Teen Assistant," and I set up Instagram, Twitter, and Facebook pages for the business. I started posting to multiple different Facebook groups about the services I was offering, and I purchased advertisements that targeted my desired audience. Gradually, my social media platforms attracted traffic and I was doing a couple of jobs a week. Clients were leaving good reviews, which naturally attracted more customers. Even with my successful start, **I had no idea where this business would eventually lead me.**

Before I knew it, I had between 25 and 40 jobs scheduled weekly, with hundreds of customers constantly texting and calling my phone. It got to the point where I would leave school right at the bell and head over to a job - and sometimes I wouldn't even get home until 10pm (I *lived* off protein bars). I had no time for my friends and family because I barely even had time for myself. There was a 3-

month period where I worked all day, every single day, without one day off in between. It was crazy, but it was exhilarating at the same time.

All of this work was too much for me to handle, but that was always something I struggled with admitting. As an entrepreneur, it's easy to feel like you have everything under control. It's easy to think you'll be able to take on every aspect of your business by yourself. But that's unrealistic. You need help - everyone does. It's hard to trust other people to maintain your quality of work, but finding those people is incredibly important. Once you establish a team of dedicated people who understand your vision and want to help you achieve it, you're golden. Don't be afraid to outsource the jobs you can't do yourself to trusted colleagues. (You'll be surprised by the abilities of other people.)

I had to take my own advice and find a team of helpful people, which consisted mainly of my peers who were looking to make some extra cash. At first, my closest friends worked for me because they were the easiest people to hire, and they seemed interested in helping out. After we did a few jobs, they realized they were making less money than I was and became frustrated with me, not understanding that the business was mine which meant I had expenses to cover. I purchased the staff uniforms, equipment needed for jobs, and handled appointment scheduling along with buying advertisements and other commodities. Even with these expenses, I paid them well above average, but they were ultimately unsatisfied with their [very generous] hourly wages. It was clearly a case of money-making envy coupled with a lack of understanding all that went into the business. This unfortunately led to the end of a few friendships which was obviously upsetting but allowed me to focus more on my business and employees who were dedicated.

Within the first year of its launch, Teen Assistant had generated over $100,000 in revenue and had over 15 full-time and part-time employees working around the clock. As our employees expanded, so did our services - at first, we only did yard jobs and moving jobs, but when our employee base grew, we were able to accommodate other jobs like tutoring and face-painting. Not only did this generate more income for the company, but it provided work to some of my peers who were uncomfortable doing physically intense jobs. Pretty soon, Teen Assistant became the go-to for all locals in search of odd jobs, and teens looking to work and earn some spending money.

Teen Assistant has been my most successful business to date, and I'm actually known around town by that name (I can't even go into a Dunkin' Donuts without someone shouting "Are you Teen Assistant?!"). Several media platforms noticed my work and reached out, which led to many features in newspapers, magazine articles, and even on television. While it was fiscally my best entrepreneurial endeavor, the lessons I learned and the connections I made through Teen Assistant were what made it my biggest success. During my few short years in high school, I had created one of the biggest businesses around town and I was receiving massive exposure. **It was surreal.**

Like all good things, my time with Teen Assistant had to come to an end. I was headed off to college and there was no feasible way I could still run the business (teens are hard enough to manage, I couldn't imagine trying to manage them from 2 hours away). Although I didn't want to say goodbye to my company, I had no other choice. I began searching for someone who could take over, and I eventually connected with another young entrepreneur in my town who was looking to purchase my business. I was sure to let him know I'd be there for background knowledge, questions, and moral support, despite being away at college. After a few meetings with him and his family, I sold Teen Assistant to him for $15,000, and that was it. Just like that, everything I'd built was in someone else's hands, and he could do whatever he wanted with it.

Luckily, he kept the same business model and Teen Assistant remains the most successful teen-run organization. Teens from my town and surrounding ones continue to provide local adults with helpful services, and the business is still incredibly strong. Though I no longer own Teen Assistant, it will always be a big part of who I am as an entrepreneur and as a person.

I am currently continuing my entrepreneurial journey at the University of Scranton where I am majoring in Entrepreneurship. I own and run various small companies, and I continue to collaborate with large brands for graphic design work. I don't know where any of my current projects will take me, but I know that one day I'm going to be one of the most successful entrepreneurs in the world. **It's just a matter of time.**

Ok, I lied. It's not a matter of time. It's a matter of extremely hard work and dedication. It's a matter of understanding what you're doing and constantly learning from it. It's a matter of caring about things. It's a matter of wanting to make everything you see just a little bit better.

In this book, I'm going to share with you everything I know about being successful, from the most unimportant details to the most crucial ones. I'm going to share my raw, honest reflections of my experiences in the big, bad business world, and I hope you'll take something from what I have to say. I hope this book opens your eyes up to your own possibilities. Like I said, I wasn't anything special. **Until I was.**

# Section I:

# YOU GOTTA WANT IT

# Chapter I:
# Why Are You Here?
## *Entrepreneurs vs. Wantrepreneurs*

Let's get something straight: there is a difference between someone who is driven by their own passion and someone who is driven by someone else's passion. An entrepreneur goes into business because he or she is fascinated and driven by something they believe in, something they love to do. A wantrepreneur goes into business in search of money - they want to profit off of things that have already proven to be successful, not things they're passionate about.

And in order to understand this difference - in order to understand why *you're* here - we need to look at the qualities of an entrepreneur.

## 1. Entrepreneurs believe in themselves.

A true entrepreneur has faith in their idea and their ability to enact it. They believe in themselves and their team. A wantrepreneur is just hoping to succeed, and only has them self in mind - they think their business revolves around them, and they don't understand the value of growth.

## 2. Entrepreneurs don't complain.

An entrepreneur is constantly taking steps forward, no matter how small. When issues arise, entrepreneurs face them head-on. Wantrepreneurs complain and look for excuses. They want things done, but they won't do it themselves.

## 3. Entrepreneurs learn from failure.

When an entrepreneur fails, they learn from it. They allow their mistakes to teach them something valuable for the future. A wantrepreneur will get discouraged by failure. Usually, it makes them want to stop altogether.

## 4. Entrepreneurs want to be the best.

The main goal of a real entrepreneur is to leave a mark on the world. They aren't concerned with the profit as much as they are with showcasing their passion. Wantrepreneurs work only for the money - they already think they're the best, and they want to be rewarded for it.

## 5. Entrepreneurs work for their business's success.

While wantrepreneurs are busy trying to make everyone think they've already succeeded, entrepreneurs are working to make real success happen. Wantrepreneurs are worried about their company's image more than its progress, and therefore rarely make time to improve the business. Entrepreneurs are always improving their business, and the image of success they create is real.

## 6. Entrepreneurs don't wait.

If there is something an entrepreneur needs, they go out and get it. Wantrepreneurs wait for things to be given to them. This often refers to funding - a wantrepreneur will only start when they're financially ready. An entrepreneur starts right away and figures things out as they go.

## 7. Entrepreneurs adapt quickly.

When things change in a business environment, a wantrepreneur will be shaken and confused, falling behind due to stress and a lack of planning. An entrepreneur is able to adapt promptly to the change and is often able to find benefits in it.

## 8. Entrepreneurs innovate.

An entrepreneur sees the world differently - they look at the ordinary and think of ways to make it extraordinary. Unlike wantrepreneurs, they don't wait for the perfect money-making idea - they search tirelessly for something the world needs, and they fulfill that necessity.

## 9. Entrepreneurs take risks.

Everyone knows that the business world can be tough, but entrepreneurs are willing to dive in head-first if it means they can change the world. Entrepreneurs don't let the possible outcomes stop them from trying. Wantrepreneurs, on the other hand, avoid risks as much as possible. They stray away from projects that might cost them more than they'll profit.

**And Most Importantly...**

## 10.    Entrepreneurs act.

Thinking of an idea is easy. Making it happen is hard. Wantrepreneurs will talk about a thousand things they want to do, but never get around to a single one. They will give up before they even start. Entrepreneurs take a single idea and put all of their time and effort into it. They act on what they say. They make things happen.

So, I want to ask you something.
Are you an entrepreneur? Do you have what it takes?

**If so, keep reading.**

# " THERE'S NO MINIMUM AGE FOR SUCCESS.

BRENDAN COX

# Chapter II:
# Age is Just a Number
### *You're never too young to be the boss.*

It takes a lot to build a successful business: patience, time, energy, money, and strategy. Because of this, many people wait until they are in college or have graduated to begin building their business. On top of that, young entrepreneurs are often discouraged from sharing their ideas due to their assumed lack of experience, knowledge, and resources. Society attempts to deter us from starting businesses because society thinks we don't know anything about business, but that's not even close to the truth.

The truth is, the corporate world isn't for everyone, but it certainly doesn't discriminate based on age. There is no set age at which you are destined to succeed, and there is no set age at which you are destined to fail. While experience, extensive knowledge, and abundant resources are certainly helpful on the path to success, they are not vital. The only thing you need to succeed is the desire to do so.

If you are young and you happen to be venturing into the business world, don't be scared. While you will feel intimidated at first, the only person who can place a limit on you is yourself. And you know yourself better than anyone else - you know your strengths, weaknesses, and ideas, and all of these things are 100% valid. Age does not correlate with value. (I had smart, qualified, college grads applying to work for Kicks Cases. They had no idea I was only 13.)

There are also many perks to becoming successful at a young age (and I'm not just talking about early retirement). You are able to enact your visions much sooner than others, which ultimately allows you to test out different ideas - kids with no worries have more room for experimentation than adults who have other lives depending on them. Also, if you happen to fail, you will have more time to learn and come back from these mistakes.

You cannot let your youth be a limitation. If you have an idea that will change the world, there is no better time to start than now. Let's take a look at some of the most successful people who didn't let their age define them:

**Mark Zuckerberg:** Founded Facebook at 19
**Bill Gates:** Founded Microsoft at age 20
**Steve Jobs:** Founded Apple at age 21
**Larry Page & Sergey Brin:** Founded Google at age 25

We know these people by their names because of the businesses they created and the impacts they had on the world. Now, I want you to imagine all of the other businesses, services, companies, and organizations that have changed the world as well. The names behind those brands come from a wide variety of age groups - there are 11 year old's making millions and 75 year old's who have just started their entrepreneurial journeys. There is no set age for an entrepreneur. There is only determination.

# Chapter III:
# Mastering Your Mindset
### *Always moving & always improving.*

Having the right mindset is critical to a successful business model. If you're not confident enough in your idea or product, you won't go very far in the business world (seriously). The thing is, it takes *a while* to master your own mindset, and there are so many different aspects to it. Don't get me wrong, nobody has the perfect outlook on life - we will all catch ourselves slipping at some point, but it's important to know where you might slip before you do.

If you're an entrepreneur like me, your mindset is focused around discovering new opportunities and making the best of them. You are constantly looking for value in the ordinary, and your eyes are always open for the next move. But what allows us to see the world like this? How are we different? What are the most important parts of an entrepreneurial mindset?

1. **Improve:** The first thing you need to clear up with yourself is the fact that **you don't know it all.** You don't. I'm sorry if that's hard for you to hear, but it's the truth for all of us. You need to understand that there is always room for improvement, and you should always be looking for it. In everything you do, there is a lesson - an opportunity to learn and practice new skills. Don't let it pass by.

2. **Accept:** There are going to be times when things don't work out exactly the way you planned. In fact, things don't usually work out as planned, but the only thing you can do is **accept it**

**and move on.** The key to staying motivated is not letting little blunders get in the way of what's really important.

3. **Stay Present:** You will not succeed if you are too concerned with the future. **Live in the moment** and worry about what's in front of you. There is no point in obsessing over the things you ultimately cannot control.

The beauty in this type of mindset is that it's a combination of things we're all capable of - qualities we have that simply need some exploring. It requires self-discipline and motivation, because you essentially have to train yourself to see things in a new way.

It takes a long time to acquire the perspective of an entrepreneur. Entrepreneurs see the world differently than other people - they are constantly looking for ways to improve themselves and the world around them. They recognize value in things that otherwise go unnoticed. Some even turn their own daily inconveniences into money-makers - the best inventions have come from entrepreneurs who successfully created something they were lacking in their lives. (We've all seen a new invention and thought "why didn't I think of that?!") But, it's important to remember that they wouldn't have achieved such status without the right mindset.

Your mindset is everything - if you aren't driven to make something happen, it never will. In order to stay motivated, always challenge yourself to make your daily life easier. Think of ways you can solve a problem around a niche you are extremely passionate about.

Without being overconfident, you have to maintain the mindset that you're going to succeed. No matter how many all-nighters, unpaid days and failures, you're going to succeed - **it's all**

**going to be worth it.** You have to be confident in yourself before anyone can put their confidence in you, so perfect your mindset now.

# THINKING
# OF AN IDEA IS
## EASY, MAKING IT
# HAPPEN IS HARD

BRENDAN COX

# Chapter IV:
# Action Over Words
## *Less talk, more action.*

Oftentimes, entrepreneurs plan their business for years and try to perfect every small detail before taking action. People will wait until they have the time, energy, money, and other resources before taking the first step. The truth is, there is no better time to start than right now. If you wait too long to enact your ideas, you'll have less of a chance of carrying through.

Talk is cheap. It's easy to make it look like you're doing a lot when all you're really doing is talking about the things you want to do. A lot of people start businesses without planning any proper course of action, and things tend to fall apart. You need to know exactly how you're going to make something happen before you tell people you're going to do it. Customers lose confidence in businesses that talk but never act.

Taking action is what sets a good entrepreneur apart. There is nothing special about saying you're going to do things - the value lies in actually doing things. Anyone can have an idea, but entrepreneurs can turn these ideas into functional and profitable realities. You are not an entrepreneur until you have enacted one of your ideas and experienced the outcome (until then, you're really just an idea-haver, which I think is kind of, like, all of us).

Here are some things to keep in mind when deciding how to take action:

- **You have a budget.** Your funds aren't limitless. Don't make any promises that don't have guaranteed financial support, and never break your bank trying to make anyone happy.

- **Limit your favors.** You might catch yourself giving too much away. Remember that you're a businessperson who is also trying to profit. If you're too generous, customers will begin to expect freebies, and your product will lose value.

- **Make it happen.** If you end up in a situation where you think you're unable to follow through on a promise, find a way. There is always a way. The worst thing you can do as an entrepreneur is disappoint eager clients.

At some point in your career, if you haven't already, you're going to bite off more than you can chew. You will agree to something you're not certain of, and you might embark on a journey you don't know anything about, and that's alright. As long as you follow through with what you say you're going to do, you're golden.

Although some may think differently, through my experience I've learned to start right away and become an expert as I go. I've had to teach myself a lot of new skills in order to continue my path, and I've made a lot of mistakes. With any business model, it's impossible to know everything before starting. So many young entrepreneurs attempt to learn every little detail and perfect everything about their business before launching it (and I understand that being a perfectionist can be a good thing), but realistically, execution is the most important part of planning your success. No matter how long you plan, it all comes down to executing your idea - **action is crucial.**

# Chapter V:
# The Best Business Are Built Around Passion
### Passion is the first step to success.

I've heard a lot of people say that monetizing your passion will take the joy out of it. People think that turning your hobby into a job kills the whole point of having a hobby. But imagine waking up every morning, excited to go to work (hard to picture for a lot of us). Who wouldn't want that?

Too often, discouraged adults end up in positions that don't satisfy them. People are forced to do jobs they don't give a crap about, and so much potential is inevitably wasted. Dreams die because people are afraid to take the risk of starting their own business. Having a career that makes you happy isn't that hard - you just have to work for something you care about.

Think of everyone you interact with on the daily and think about their faces. Do they seem happy? When your parents come home at the end of the day, are they excited to tell you about work? When you check out at the grocery store, does the cashier seem happy? When you pass police officers and construction workers, are they smiling? Are the people you know actually satisfied with their careers, their lives? Or do they wish they were in another field?

The sad truth is that most of us don't end up with careers that make us happy. A lot of people end up doing things they couldn't care less about. They'll watch the clock all week, anxiously waiting for the weekend, and their weekends are filled with dread for the upcoming week. It's a long, sad cycle that lasts forever, and it shouldn't have to be this way.

Starting a business out of passion is crucial to the longevity of your business. With every step you take, you need to think about yourself - every decision you make should involve asking yourself "Will I care about this a year from now?" If you don't think it's something you'll care about in the future, it's probably not something worth doing.

The key to a successful and happy life is loving what you do (yes, I realize how cliché that sounds, but it's true). There is no joy in watching the clock and dreading the passage of time - the joy lies in deciding where your time goes. Being an entrepreneur means creating your *own* clock and looking forward to each passing minute.

# Chapter VI:
# Identify Your Target Market
### *Who are you trying to appeal to?*

Once you've identified your passions and interests, you need to decide which part of the market you will fit into. Honestly, this part can be tough because of how unique and individual you are. Categorizing yourself under a certain niche can be intimidating and cause a lot of pressure. It might even paralyze you into inaction, but you can't let it.

Your niche should reflect your specialty - you should aim your products and services at an audience who has a realistic chance of investing in you. For example, if you're into fitness, you should target consumers in the health and fitness niche for the best chance of success. With today's technology, you can advertise to your ideal customer - you can literally build your perfect client and many social media platforms will find those people and put your product on their timelines. You have nothing to lose by selecting a niche.

But what if you don't know what you're into? What if your interests don't necessarily fit into any certain category?

**Start anyway.** Hit the ground running. It is better to identify a niche and absolutely, completely, 100% fail than to never even start at all. This way, you know what works and what doesn't. You know what you're not cut out for. With experience in multiple different niches, you can test out ideas, learn from your mistakes, and ultimately enter the market sooner than you would have. There is nothing wrong with experimentation.

There's clearly a niche for everyone (I mean, think about some of the things you've seen advertisements for. If there's a niche for phone fans and selfie lights, there's a niche for you). Once you find the part of the market that you belong in, it's important to fully analyze and understand it.

In order to create a profitable business, you need to think of the problems that people in your target audience are experiencing, and you need to assess your ability to fix them. Being a businessperson is being able to tell clients what they need before they know it themselves, and there are so many ways to interact with your clients nowadays.

- **Initiate one-on-one conversations.** This is the most effective way to gather ideas.

- **Explore online forums.** Take a look at the questions being asked and the issues being raised.

- **Research!** You should always be uncovering new information about your niche.

Another important part of understanding your specific niche is understanding its profitability. An effective way to assess this is to browse the top products and services in your category, and price your own products and services accordingly. It is also beneficial to research your competition so you can understand what you're up against - your ultimate goal is being the best of your kind.

Above all, you can't give up until you've tried it all. Entrepreneurship is a learning curve for everyone, so don't be discouraged if you're struggling to find the right niche. On top of that, don't let a rocky start get you down - if you've picked a niche and you just can't seem to get it right, be sure to perfect your advertising. Make sure you're taking the necessary steps to reach your audience, and make sure your audience consists of the right people. Sometimes, business will slow down because the right people simply can't find you - not because they don't need you. Having a niche and working it to the maximum is making sure you're never hidden from people who want to find you.

**66**

# AN IDEA WITHOUT EXECUTION IS DESTINED FOR FAILURE. **99**

BRENDAN COX

# Chapter VII:
# Execution Over Everything
## *An idea is just the beginning.*

Like I said before, there is nothing special about having an idea. Even if it's the best idea in the world, it needs a lot of planning and careful execution to ever be worth it. Too often, potential is wasted on ideas that just sit on the backburner because no one can figure out how to make anything happen. The thing is, there's always a way to make something happen. **Good entrepreneurs execute.**

A proper execution plan involves motivated people who understand the vision and want to make it a reality. If your team isn't stacked with intelligent and resourceful people, you won't be able to execute your idea. You need people who are excited to make the next move.

Similarly, you need people who do things the right way - there is no room for shortcuts. If you or your team doesn't know exactly how to get something done, research until you get it right. There is no point in creating extra work for yourself by taking a shortcut that could have easily been avoided. If you find yourself having to take shortcuts at all, your business model probably isn't ready.

An important way to make sure you're executing your ideas in the right way is to ensure that your business is optimizing its value for everyone involved. You are executing your idea successfully if everyone is satisfied - customers, employees, vendors, and yourself. A good business gives back what it takes from its participants.

Everyone involved with your business should theoretically be able to run it on their own. Your team should be just as invested as you are because the whole team is responsible for providing a satisfactory experience. Also, it is beneficial to have employees that comprehend and replicate your visions in the event that someone else may need to step up in times of crisis.

That said, times of crisis should not be the only instances in which the business model is reconsidered. A large part of execution is planning for unexpected obstacles, even if they don't yet exist. Not only does this allow your business to adapt to changes when they do occur, but it also allows you to move past those changes much quicker than other businesses and gives you time for new opportunities.

## Pro Tip: With a new business model, think of one "worst case scenario" and how you'd fix it.

Finally, when executing your business, always remember that communication is key. Your business will gradually expand, and one day it may be too much for you to control all by yourself. You need to establish steady communication between all branches of your organization, so the customer's experience remains constant no matter what. Strong communication becomes more challenging when more people are involved, but it's crucial to stay in touch. Set expectations for your team and let them know when those expectations aren't met. Everyone involved in your business should be accepting of feedback from customers and from you.

Execution is hands-down the hardest part of running a successful company. It takes years to perfect the ins-and-outs of your business model, and you're probably never going to have it perfect. However, there are so many little steps you can take to ensure your business continues to improve. Execute, and never stop executing.

# Chapter VIII:
# Commitment is Key
## *Devote yourself entirely to your business.*

Success doesn't happen overnight. It takes hard work and dedication - you need to wake up each morning and commit to your success all over again. In order to make sure you stay on the right path, you constantly have to remind yourself about the purpose of your startup. Each day should teach you something about why you're in business, and each choice you make should be a committed decision.

The first commitment you have to make is to your idea. If what you're pursuing doesn't feel right in your heart, it probably isn't right. For a business to succeed, people need to commit wholeheartedly to its entire existence. It's like having a kid (kind of?): if you don't have the time, energy, resources, and passion to keep a business alive, you probably shouldn't even have one. A business is not something you can work on only when you feel like it - it should be your whole life. You get out of your business exactly what you put into it - if you aren't committed to your success, there is no reason for anyone else to be. Your business needs everything you've got.

Among fully committing to your success, there are tons of other little commitments you need to make along the way. Allowing a business to become your entire life involves making sacrifices, and if you can't commit to those sacrifices and understand why you have to make them, you won't be satisfied. Entrepreneurs have to compromise with many other aspects of their life - sometimes, having a business life can mean giving up your personal life. For some, this sounds extreme but for us, this is normal. **For us, business is personal.**

Another aspect of commitment is taking responsibility for your actions - the failure or success of your startup is linked directly to you. Good entrepreneurs take the ultimate leadership position and all of the responsibilities that come with it - a business failure is a personal failure, and a business success is a personal success. The best thing you can do in either case is learn and get better.

A good entrepreneur, while keeping their business in mind, is not afraid to explore the unknown to further their success. In entrepreneurship, taking calculated risks is extremely important and can be very rewarding, but these risks require strong commitment just like anything else. If you think a risk is worth taking, consider it carefully until your mind is made up. Risks are some of the biggest commitments you can make, and you can't turn around once you start.

Above all, understand that each day is a new commitment to your success. Know that your business is nothing without you. Remember your goal, your vision, your purpose. Commit to making yourself and your business better. You cannot change your mind once you dive in - your only option is to swim to the other side.

# Chapter IX:
# You Don't Know It All.
## *If you can't take advice, you don't deserve it.*

When you have a network of people committed to your success, you can bet they'll have opinions about it. As an entrepreneur, you're going to be bombarded with other people's ideas - people who have something to say about what you're doing. It can be annoying, but the best way to improve is to listen to those around you (some people straight up have no idea what they're talking about, but some do).

Every person you meet can be a mentor to you in some way, and I'll bet you have countless mentors in your life already. Your relatives, teachers, friends, colleagues - they all bring irreplaceable value to your life that ultimately shapes who you are. Without the lessons you've learned from these people, you wouldn't have even come this far so they're definitely worth something.

Even if everyone in your life isn't involved in your business, there is a lesson you can learn from them. There are always going to be people with more life experience than you, and it's important to take advantage of the opportunities you have to learn from them. It's easy to think you already have all the knowledge you need, but there is always room for improvement.

You're going to receive a lot of advice from many different people. Some of it's going to be crap, but a lot of it will be valuable information. Sometimes, people think they know everything about you and your business and will think they can give you the best advice when they really can't. Regardless of how useful it may be to you, always be accepting of advice from others. Gather all the advice

51

people give you and analyze what you think is worthy of implementing into your business.

Learning to take criticism is just as important as learning to take advice. There is always going to be someone who disagrees with what you're doing or thinks you're doing it the wrong way. Not a single person on Earth has everyone's approval, and that's okay. Handling criticism is a healthy way to ensure that you are always bettering yourself and your business. If you can't face the facts, your success isn't a reality.

Entrepreneurship is a learning curve, and I will say that a thousand times if I need to. If you are not ready to learn and grow, there is no reason for you to be here. Understanding that you can always expand your knowledge is the first step to success.

# Chapter X:
# Trust Your Gut.
## *Don't second guess yourself.*

At the end of the day, you know yourself best. You know your ideas and goals, and you know your abilities. There is no one else who can tell you how *you* can succeed.

These days, with advanced technology and information at our fingertips, it can feel like every decision we make is based on some kind of algorithm. Our most important life decisions - relationships, job applications, big purchases - are made with the click of a button, and the world is losing a lot of its authenticity.

Amidst a modern age that begs you to trust everything you read on your smartphone, you need to remember the value, accuracy, and importance of your gut instincts. Your body and brain have a way of processing the information around you that shouldn't be questioned.

Fun fact: 4 in 10 CEOs say they still make decisions based on intuition, despite having access to loads of numerical data. Intuition is the result of your body's own algorithms processing the millions of little signals it receives each day. Don't get me wrong, there is still immense value in numbers - we will always rely on data, but we should rely on ourselves a little more.

Understanding the inner workings of your gut instinct can be helpful in identifying the feeling you get when you make a decision. Your body likely has its own, personalized way of letting you know you're in an uncomfortable situation (for me, my stomach tightens up). It's important to recognize that feeling when it occurs, and make your next decision based on that information.

All throughout your business career, you are going to interact with different people, and you are going to have to analyze their intentions. For instance, you might meet someone who approaches you as a supportive equal but is really trying to tap into your success and make a buck off you. Know that when someone feels shifty, they probably are.

Another thing to remember when going with your gut is the impermanence of trends. When the hottest new product comes around, it's easy to want to hop on the bandwagon because it's proving successful for others. Stats and other empirical evidence will probably bombard you with that same proof of success. I know it's tempting but resist the opportunities that seem like quick money-makers - they'll probably end up tiring out.

There is no perfect process for decision making - decisions are well thought-out compilations of instinct and fact. I can't say for sure that one is more accurate than the other, but I can say that your gut rarely fails you. Whether you make an instant decision or a prolonged one, listening to your gut is the best thing you can do. You know what is best for yourself and your business, and you can't let anyone tell you otherwise.

# Section II:

# PUSH THROUGH

# IF YOU DON'T HAVE HATERS YOU'RE DOING SOMETHING WRONG.

BRENDAN COX

# Chapter I:
# Pleasing Everyone.
## *Do for you. Not for others.*

Let's face it - you can't please everyone (but I can see the logic behind wanting to). Many entrepreneurs have the idea that if they satisfy more needs or address more problems, their market will be bigger. In a perfect world this would be true, but in our world, trying to get everyone's approval is a fast track to failure.

Instead of running around trying to put a smile on everyone's face, focus on what puts a smile on yours. Identify the things you're passionate about and follow them. In business, it's better to go *beyond the expectations* of a small population than to *simply appeal* to a larger one. You are never going to find a business that a) pleases everyone, b) makes millions, and c) hasn't already been done. If you're still looking for one of those, stop putting so much pressure on yourself - choose a business *you're* interested in, not just something you think a lot of others would be interested in.

Today's market is full of business opportunities and chances to climb to the top. Customers are looking for someone who is the best at what they do - you are aiming to satisfy needs better than other companies. In other words, pick something to do and give your absolute best to your target market. Focus on pleasing them first.

You should always remain conscious of your current circumstances before trying to outdo yourself. Utilize your resources without exhausting them - remember that you have a budget and a plan to follow, so try to steer clear of things that might flip your world upside down. Don't move mountains trying to deliver a positive experience - if customers truly support you, they shouldn't need much convincing.

If you think customers are the only ones who will give you a run for your money, you're mistaken. Believe it or not, your very own entrepreneurial partners will likely want to see you fail before you get bigger than them. When you start to look like you're doing well, people get jealous - some may bash you, some may steal your ideas, and some may just make you feel really crappy. Despite it all, you need to keep your composure. Make friends with everyone and don't let potential competition know about your weaknesses.

At the end of the day, don't let any of it get to you. That's the most valuable thing I can tell you. There are always going to be people who don't agree with you, or think you're doing it all wrong, or would love nothing more than to see you fail. Remember why you're here and who you're here for.

# Chapter II:
# Failure is a Good Thing
## *& you can't avoid it.*

I hate to break it to you, but …

At some point in your life, in some aspect of your life, you are going to fail. I know it sounds scary, but failure is inevitable. It happens to everyone.

As humans, we are preconditioned to avoid failure because we associate it with negativity and pain - our society views failure as a sign of weakness and defeat. We break our backs trying to keep ourselves afloat because no one has ever told us it's OK to sink sometimes. People may tell you, "Take risks!" or "Put yourself out there!", but you've probably never heard anyone tell you to make mistakes, so that's why I'm here.

If you're not making mistakes, you're not working hard enough. Mistakes are the result of an attempt to get something right - they show how hard you're working to fine-tune your idea. As an entrepreneur, it's important to create a business environment that accepts and encourages mistakes. Everyone makes mistakes, but good entrepreneurs see the educational value in them.

Those who make mistakes learn more than those who don't. If you never test an idea because you're afraid to fail, you will never know what works and what doesn't. On the other hand, if you test every idea you have, you're bound to make mistakes but you're also bound to find out what's effective. For example, a social media influencer can't guarantee their first post will go viral - it could take hundreds of tries for them to figure out what appeals to their audience, but if they stop posting, they'll never know. It's impossible to recognize improvement if you've never known the opposite.

Failure also allows you a chance to step back, reassess, and develop a proper strategy for overcoming it. If you never allow yourself to fail, you won't know how to come back from it when it finally happens. Understanding your mistakes and learning how to fix them is an essential part of being an entrepreneur - when obstacles arise, you should have a detailed plan on how to get around them.

That being said, it's a lot better to fail early because it's more dangerous to fail later in the game. When you're older, more depends on you and more is at stake. You will likely have an entire family to support, finances to protect, and necessities to maintain - your decisions will affect more than just yourself. Alternatively, when you're young and just starting out, failure is more beneficial than it is detrimental - your only way is up.

I speak from experience. When I was in seventh grade, I had an Instagram account dubbed @WorstCalls with over 400,000 followers. It had a sports niche and featured the worst calls from sports games, and it was the top of its kind. One morning, I woke up to an email that my account had been suspended due to, in no specific terms, a violation of Instagram guidelines. I tried and tried to get the account back, but I ultimately lost that account and all of its followers. It was obviously a big loss, both financially and emotionally, but it only motivated me more. I didn't let that loss affect my desire to be successful on Instagram, so I simply put it behind me and moved on.

The best advice I can give here is to never let your failures stop you from trying again. Your life is a series of decisions - some of them will be right and some of them won't. You are bound to take the wrong turn at some point, it just can't stop you from moving.

# COMPETITION FORCES YOU TO WORK HARDER.

BRENDAN COX

# Chapter III:
# Competition
## *It's your biggest motivator.*

I know it's hard to believe, but competition is healthy for business. When there is nothing to compete with, you stop striving for improvement and become comfortable with your position. But when someone is always trying to be better than *you*, you're motivated to be better than *them*.

Competition inspires you to innovate - the goal is to come up with something bigger and better than the other businesses. You should always be looking for ways to stand out from your rivals. If you aren't constantly improving your business, you will start to blend in with the rest of the crowd and your competitors will take over. Pay attention to what your competitors lack and use that as ammunition for your next idea.

Think ahead of your competition. Watch trends and other businesses closely and stay one step ahead of everything in your industry. Try to be the leader and not the follower. Consumers often choose the company that is continuously adjusting their business to keep up with technology and today's world. You cannot be successful if you remain unchanged.

Another important tip: Don't obsess over your competition. There is no point in worrying about the things you can't control - your competition is going to exist no matter what you do. Instead of wasting time worrying about your rivalries, spend that time thinking of ways to be better than them. Stop being jealous of them and start making them jealous of you. Do everything in your power to get to the top.

Don't get me wrong, competition sucks. If it were up to me, we'd all have our own million-dollar industry and no one would have to worry about anyone else. The fact of the matter is, we *all* want to be the best and there is *always* going to be something or someone else trying to stop us. The key to being a good entrepreneur is seeing your competition as your motivation - recognize those who are doing better than you, learn from them, and then surpass them.

# Chapter IV:
# Never Clock Out
## *This is a 24-hour job.*

Entrepreneurs don't have a typical 40-hour work week - our jobs are never ending. Whether we're in the office or not, our minds are constantly racing with new ideas, next objectives, and upcoming projects. There is no beginning and there is no end - being an entrepreneur means a 24/7 commitment to your business.

The average corporate workday, your typical "9 to 5," starts and ends roughly at the same time each day - and people eagerly await the minute they get in their cars to go home. Once they're home, they don't think about their job until the next morning - they don't remain inspired by their work. They just dread the ring of the alarm clock.

Entrepreneurs, on the other hand, can't wait to wake up in the morning. They're excited to continue their work and keep improving - the passage of time doesn't scare off a real entrepreneur. Time is our biggest advantage, and we need to use it wisely.

The best thing you can do as an entrepreneur is maximize your time. There are people who are perfectly content with working for a set number of hours and then relaxing. Those people choose to budget their time between work and home. An entrepreneur needs to merge their work and home life so the two become one - your work is your lifestyle, and your downtime at home should be used to further your business.

There is always something you could be doing. When you're lounging around watching TV, challenge yourself to watch something educational that pertains to your life as a businessperson. Before you close all the tabs on your computer and relax for the night, browse the internet for new ideas that you could implement into your business. Even if the best thing you can do is practice your problem-solving customer service skills on your family, you should always be looking for ways to advance your knowledge.

Your success depends directly on how much time you put into it. If your workday ends at all, you're not passionate enough about what you're doing. Good entrepreneurs carry their business through every aspect of their lives - we wake up each day with a desire to improve, and we go to bed each night better than we were before.

# Chapter V:
# How to Handle Stress
### *Don't let it eat you up.*

Entrepreneurs spend their lives making sacrifices to reach their goals, which inevitably comes with a lot of stress. Many people associate the word "success" with money, happiness, and luxury. For a true entrepreneur, the reality of success is hard work, long hours, and a whole lot of hurdles to jump before we get to where we want to be. Stress management is an essential skill for entrepreneurs. Running a successful business can be extremely tough, and you might find yourself feeling overwhelmed. In order to succeed in the business world, you need to know how to take control of your stress and turn it into positive energy that you can use to advance your business.

## 1. Simplify problems

It's impossible to tackle a problem you don't understand. Sometimes, in business, multiple problems will arise at once at it'll feel like everything is falling apart - take a step back and identify the root of your issues. More often than not, multiple little problems are created out of *one original problem* that needs a simple fix. Understanding where your business is falling short will help you to eliminate future issues, and therefore future stress.

## 2. Do things you like to do

At the end of the day, the person you're trying to please is yourself. Although it's tempting to put your needs behind your business, you have to remember that your business is nothing without you. If you're not happy, you ultimately won't succeed. Make time in your busy schedule to do things that genuinely spark joy in you, whether it relates to your business or not. You can't create the best version of your business until you're the best version of yourself.

## 3. It's OK to take a break

Entrepreneurs are born with a constant, undying desire to hustle. We're always moving - a lot of us would probably turn down the opportunity to take a break, but we need to remember that we deserve it. No one can be expected to perform one hundred percent of the time, so take a breather every once in a while. If you start to feel stressed out, clear your head for a few minutes. Take a nap. Go for a walk. It's OK to put something on pause and come back to it later.

## 4. Learn to say no

If you're like me, you probably don't like to disappoint anyone. You want to make sure you satisfy everyone that reaches out to you, even if you can't. You might even agree to something crazy just so you don't have to say no. But it's unrealistic to provide everything for everyone. If something is out of your comfort zone, or it's really just too much to handle, *say no*. Turn down the offer. Your skills aren't going anywhere, but your sanity might.

## 5. Stay calm

When you're an entrepreneur, you're in control of your life. Whatever problem you're facing, it's probably not the end of the world. There is no point in freaking out over things that have simple solutions, especially when you're your own boss. Stay focused and keep your eyes on the ultimate prize: **success.**

# Chapter VI:
# Be Realistic
## *Lower your expectations, plan don't dream.*

As an entrepreneur, you need to know how to set realistic goals for yourself. Having a business is exciting, but people don't always understand what they're signing up for. Entrepreneurship is not a one-way ticket to success - it's a long and hard process that involves implementing and monetizing your own skills in the best way possible.

Entrepreneurs tend to feel like they can do everything themselves, and it's often hard for us to hear that we *can't* do something. Confidence is key, but you can't let it get the best of you. While we should all be proud of what we're good at, that's not where the money is. Money, fame, and success come from being the best at something - everyone can be good, but only one can be the best.

That being said, becoming the best takes a whole team of people. No one can be good at everything, let alone do everything on their own. We all need some help. It's important to be aware of your strengths and weaknesses - outsource the things you can't accomplish on your own. Hire a skilled team. This way, you can improve upon your skills and allow others to improve upon theirs, all while reducing your workload.

Along with being realistic about your abilities, you need to be realistic about your finances. Don't make plans or promises that can't be financially supported. In other words, don't count on things you can't afford - if you get your hopes up about something that's not in the budget, you'll always find yourself disappointed. You should always be aware of your business' budget, and you should keep detailed financial records, so you know where your money is going.

All business decisions should be made with money in mind - there is a difference between wanting your business to be able to afford something, and your business actually being able to afford something (it sounds silly, but it's a significant issue in the business world). Don't sign up for something you know isn't possible.

An important way to stay realistic is to plan one thing at a time and stop dreaming. You can't allow yourself to be influenced by others' successes - everyone is on their own unique journey, and it's more important to plan your next step than to keep fantasizing about your ultimate goal. You reach your goals with planning and execution - there is no magic formula for success, even though it seems like that these days. Don't compare yourself to others - stay in your own lane and focus on your next objective. Plan, don't dream.

# Chapter VII:
# Success Doesn't Happen Overnight
### *Patience is a virtue.*

The most common obstacle in becoming successful is thinking it'll happen overnight. Whether you're an entrepreneur or not, most of us have an unconscious desire to succeed without putting in work, which defeats us a lot quicker than hard work. It's dangerous to believe you are going to wake up one day and be where you want to be, because you're going to be disappointed every morning.

These days, our life goals are so heavily impacted by what we see others doing. The internet is full of people who financially and physically "have it all," and it's easy to let yourself assume they're not working hard for it. Scrolling through your feed becomes a contest between who has the nicest things rather than genuine information about what people are up to. When all we see are images of what success looks like, we never see the process of actually achieving it - what goes on behind the scenes is completely foreign to us.

The reason we don't see it is because it's ugly. The road to success is uphill and bumpy, but there's no way around it. In order to succeed, you have to go through a strenuous process full of ups and downs, and there is never any guarantee. Success depends directly on how much work you're willing to put in - if you aren't willing to make it happen, it won't happen.

A lot of things that seem like overnight successes are really just things that you hear about once they are already successful. Just because you're only hearing about them now doesn't mean they don't have years of trial and error behind them. Some of our favorite companies went through years of disappointment before they got any attention. Take a look:

- Microsoft was founded in 1975 but didn't go public until 1986. Bill Gates spent 11 years perfecting his "overnight success."

- Apple was established in 1976 but struggled until the later 90s when the Mac was invented. Steve Jobs worked on his "overnight success" for over two decades.

- Google started in 1996 but no one really heard about it until 2004. Larry Page and Sergey Brin's "overnight success" took 8 years.

- Facebook (originally "Facemash") was launched in 2003 as the result of Mark Zuckerberg's college breakup. It cost him millions of dollars, until it eventually became an "overnight success" 5 years later.

- Amazon.com was founded in 1994 by Jeff Bezos, who didn't expect a hefty profit. It became public 3 years later and is now an "overnight success" with over 112 million users.

**Overnight success isn't real.** Success comes from years of hard work and dedication. You're not going to wake up one day and magically be successful, so you better keep working.

STAY HUNGRY STAY HUMBLE

BRENDAN COX

# Chapter VIII:
# Stay Motivated
## *Always Hungry.*

Entrepreneurs are born with a natural drive for business, but it can be challenging to stay motivated. Sometimes, entrepreneurs achieve their version of success and decide they've done enough - too many businesspeople waste their potential by gradually falling off the map. A true entrepreneur knows that their work is never done.

A common idea among people who are just entering the business world is that there is some kind of finish line - a point you eventually reach, above everyone else, where there is nothing to do but bask in your glory. People think their only task is to get to the top, just so they can look down at everyone else - they're **extrinsically** driven. Entrepreneurs are driven by their own **intrinsic** motivation to continue learning and improving.

Motivation is tricky - at our lowest, we tend to lose our motivation because we've lost sight of the light at the end of the tunnel. Conversely, when life is good, we tend to become complacent where we are - we stop seeing any need for improvement. The key, in either situation, is to remember this: there is always something you can do to make your situation better. Most entrepreneurs don't even have to hear this, but you're a *long* way from being able to stop. You should *never* stop.

You have to stay hungry. Entrepreneurs are never at rest - we are constantly on lookout for the next big thing. There is no excuse for complacency. In a world that is always changing, there will always be a new opportunity for success and we have to take advantage of those chances. Otherwise, we're wasting our time on this planet. We were blessed with a natural desire to create, innovate, and make an impact, and we have to feed that desire endlessly.

# Chapter IX:
# **Adapt & Overcome**
### *Problems are inevitable.*

Let's face it - things don't always work out as planned. There are going to be multiple instances where you find yourself needing to make a new plan. Entrepreneurs face a lot (and I mean A LOT) of unforeseen issues throughout our careers, and we need to know how to handle them. "Improvise, Adapt, Overcome" is the unofficial slogan of the U.S. Marines, and it's used to emphasize the importance of reacting properly to unexpected changes in combat.

I know we're not fighting any battles, but we entrepreneurs should keep that slogan in the back of our minds at all times. Entrepreneurs need to develop a mindset that is comfortable with uncertainty - things are always changing, and nothing is ever certain. If you are uncomfortable with the possibility of change, you are not ready to be an entrepreneur.

Before you can truly embark on your entrepreneurial journey, your mindset should be strong enough for adaptation. The most important ability you can have as an entrepreneur is the ability to adapt without becoming unstable. Businesses fail most often due to unpredicted challenges that test their stability. You always have to be prepared for the possibility that something goes wrong so that you know how to fix it when it does.

When an issue arises, don't panic. The last thing you should do when something goes wrong is freak out (which I know, sometimes you can't control). Try to compose yourself and think of a plan of action to fix the problem and prevent it from happening in the future. Obviously, this is easier said than done, but the best way to handle unexpected challenges is by breaking down the issue and finding the root of it. Sometimes, multiple issues are stemming from one source - identify the source and either cut it off or address it. This way, you won't face the same problem again.

Fixing the problem is important, but it is just as important to learn and grow from what occurred. In order to improve yourself and your business, you need to analyze your own courses of action, and take note of what's effective. This is where the "overcoming" part comes in - if you don't learn from your challenges, you will not grow as an entrepreneur. Remember what works and what doesn't. Keep track of the hurdles you jump and use the same form every time.

# Chapter X:
# Fight Fear
## *Stop letting fear limit you.*

The biggest obstacle entrepreneurs face is our own fear - the intensity of the business world puts a lot of pressure on us. Every decision we make affects the future of our business, so it is natural to be hesitant when taking chances. I understand how scary the corporate world can be, but you can't escape the intimidation. Fear follows us everywhere, but a good entrepreneur persists in spite of it.

The business world sees a lot of failure - a lot of ideas come and go, and many ventures fail before they get off the ground. The survival rate of startups is alarmingly low, and this constant threat of failure looms over entrepreneurs indefinitely. Sometimes, these fears even prevent potential entrepreneurs from venturing out and exploring their interests. You have a greater possibility for success once you stop letting your fears control you - instead, **control your fear.**

Entrepreneurs tend to worry most about losing their best important clients and consequently running out of money, and this fear acts as a motivator for many of us. The key to being successful in a profession that demands your full commitment is not only to take control of your fears, but to use them as motivation for improvement. For instance, the fear of losing your best clients should motivate you to improve your customer experience - it shouldn't stop you from working.

You also have to understand that losing customers and losing money is a natural part of business. As an entrepreneur, you will have many wins and many losses - losing is a part of every game, and it definitely shouldn't stop you from playing. There is always a chance that something won't go the way you want it to - investing your hard-earned money into any aspect of a business is always uncertain. Even so, you should take risks. With every chance something will go wrong, there is the chance it will go right.

For entrepreneurs (or anyone, really), fear is inevitable. There is no correct way to respond to the fear of failure - some work harder to make it disappear, and others ignore it completely. Whether fear drives you to improve or simply follows you around, allowing fear to hold you back from your highest potential should never be an option. It may try to push you down, but no matter what you do, you have to push back.

"SUCCEEDING IN THE BUSINESS WORLD HAS SO MUCH TO DO WITH MAKING CONNECTIONS. IT'S MORE ABOUT WHO YOU KNOW THAN WHAT YOU KNOW"

BRENDAN COX

# Chapter I:
# Stay Connected
## *Succeeding in the business world heavily revolves around making connections.*

The biggest names in the corporate world have huge networks of people standing behind them - people who support the ideas and goals of the business. As an entrepreneur, it's important to build stable relationships with everyone you meet because you never know how they might be able to help you in the future. You should always remember to be kind, respectful, and helpful to the people you come across. You need to build strong, long term relationships with as many people as you can because one day, you'll need your network of supporters.

On top of making good impressions, you should try to get the phone numbers, emails, and social media handles of everyone you meet. In today's world, technology enables us to make connections instantly, especially through the power of social media. With a few simple taps, you can be in touch with anyone and uncover anything about them - LinkedIn, Facebook, Instagram, Twitter, you name it.

It's important to keep your own social media pages looking clean and professional so you can use them to score potential business opportunities. Your platforms should be attractive and informational, and people should never have to try super hard to find you. It's also crucial to maintain a presence on your social platforms - you should post consistently and routinely interact with other posts. This will boost the activity on your pages and consequently within your business.

Every day, as part of my daily routine I reach out to over 40 new entrepreneurs. I value making connections and relationships. With today's technology, there's absolutely no excuse for not wanting to make connections. Twenty years ago, you had to go to conventions and shake people's hands and talk to them (crazy, right?). In today's modern society, you can send someone a direct message, email them or connect with them on LinkedIn. Set aside at least 20 minutes every day to make connections. Trust me, it's worth it.

You should create connections that will benefit you and your business in the future. The most successful people have a specific person they can contact for assistance in each aspect of their business (you know, those people who have "a guy" for everything). Your connections allow you to build a network of intelligent individuals who are passionate about your business and bring value to it daily. Running a business becomes so much easier with dependable people at every turn - connections should never be underestimated.

# Chapter II:
# Stay Current with Trends
## *Keep an eye on patterns.*

Entrepreneurs are constantly on the lookout for new opportunities, and a big part of that is keeping up with trends. New ideas are always circulating in the business world, and it's impossible to know what's going to be hip or popular at a given point in time. There is so much creativity in the world, and we have to keep our eyes open for it - the next big thing can happen at any time, and we can't risk missing it.

One way to make sure you stay current with trends is by keeping up with social media. It provides instant access to loads of public information that can help you grow your business. Most social media platforms even have a designated section where you can explore what is currently "trending." The news is another great way to stay up to date with new progressions in the market - there are hundreds of news sources dedicated entirely to providing information about business analytics.

The crazy thing is, hopping on a trend early enough can literally be the defining factor in your success. Don't get me wrong, I don't recommend desperately chasing a trend that doesn't necessarily suit your passions, but there is rarely any harm in testing out a new idea. The example I like to use is Fidget Spinners - obviously, spinney stress-relieving objects aren't really anyone's passion, but those who hopped on the trend early enough are millionaires now. They're set for life just because they saw an opportunity and took it.

Trends have always been (and are always going to be) big money makers - they're usually the hottest new thing that everyone wants. Consumers tend to make impulsive purchases in the heat of a new movement because, like us entrepreneurs, they're determined to stay relevant. The best way to stay relevant is to stay current - you can't make money off of things you don't pay attention to.

# Chapter III:
# Social Media is Everything
## *Maximize your social media presence.*

No matter how you feel about it, social media has become an absolute staple in our everyday lives. It is embedded in every aspect of our existence, which is why it is a great way for entrepreneurs to stay connected. Having a social media presence comes with numerous benefits for the entrepreneurial community - the internet is a place for everyone to grow, for free.

Keeping up with your social media platforms naturally creates a presence for your business. Your business should have its own page where you post content that will not only promote your services but offer value to your customers. You should create a steady but realistic posting schedule - when you post consistently, you establish yourself as a thought leader, and you lay the foundation for your business "personality." You also stay fresh in your clients' minds - people are on social media every day, so you should be too.

Every one of your followers should be following you for a reason. People don't usually gravitate towards accounts that are inactive or boring. Your content should allow current clients and potential customers to find their place within your company - people tend to develop emotional connections to social media pages, so your posts should be compelling, thought-provoking, and interesting to look at. You should also encourage your followers to interact by inviting their opinions and commenting back. Creating a dialogue with your audience is extremely important - no one knows your customers better than themselves.

I often get asked, "How do I know what to post?" or "What do my followers want to see?" The answer is, *you have to think of your audience as yourself*. What would *you* want to see on your feed? What catches *your* attention? Your audience is primarily composed of a bunch of people who are just like you - your customers are people who care about what you're doing. Their minds work like yours, so it shouldn't be too difficult to come up with appealing content.

Another great thing about social media is that if you don't already have your target audience, you can easily find it. Many different platforms allow you to purchase targeted advertising in which you can create posts directed at a certain demographic. Your posts will show up on the timelines of people who might be interested, and you can easily locate potential clients this way. This is why it's important to keep your page looking clean and fresh - the first impression is usually the most important.

In general, social media is a great way to make sure you're always working. Even if you're laying down in bed, you can be making progress on your social media platforms. Whether you are creating your next posts, reaching out to other entrepreneurs, or interacting with your audience, keeping up with your social media ensures that your business maintains a presence. As our world continues to evolve, social media seems to be the one thing staying constant. It's not going away, so you'd better get used to it - it's your most useful tool.

# Chapter IV:
# How to Be Talked About
## *Word of mouth is crucial.*

While it's important to maintain a positive reputation on social media, your business should also have a positive reputation in the real world. Your business should stay in the back of people's minds, even when they're not thinking of you directly - everyday life should start to remind people of you and your services. Your goal is to grow your business to the point where you become the first option when people need something.

Word of mouth has always been and will always be the best, most effective way to grow a business - people talk. If someone likes what you're doing, you can almost always count on them telling people about it. And on top of that, people are way more likely to check out your business if they hear about it from someone they trust. This is why it's so important to leave a good impression - you can bet on being the talk of the town.

Creating a message or experience that is remarkable enough to be talked about isn't always an easy task. Here are a few tips on how to keep a positive reputation and make sure the word-of-mouth is all good things.

## 1. You should exceed expectations

Your focus as a business owner is satisfying your customers. Not only should you meet the expectations you set forth for your clients, but you should go above and beyond them. A few extra details can make all the difference when someone reflects on their experience with your business. Every time you interact with a customer, you should leave them feeling surprised and inspired - you want to make people say "wow," because those are the customers that go off and tell everyone about it.

## 2. It should be easy to leave reviews

The same way it's easy for unhappy customers to leave bad reviews, it should be easy for your supporters to say nice things about your business. On your social media pages (Facebook, Yelp), make sure your review settings are turned on so people can leave star ratings. Your website should also have a designated comment section where people can leave details about their experience. You should be checking these reviews and responding to concerns as necessary - your customers' feedback is incredibly important.

## 3. You should promote through PR

Developing public relations helps to keep your business in the public eye. It's important to create and maintain stable relationships with other local businesspeople like journalists, radio stations, newspapers, and online influencers. This is the best way to keep people up to date with your future business plans. Also, you should be present in your community - if you aren't hosting your own events, you should be attending others. This is a great way to meet new people and make new connections.

# Chapter V:
# You Are Your Business
*You represent your business on and off the clock.*

As the founder, owner, and primary runner, you have the responsibility of representing your business in each aspect of your life. You should be the living, breathing embodiment of your business, which means you have to live your life by the same morals and values you project through your brand. Actions you take in your daily life *can* and *will* affect your business's view in the public eye, so you kind of have to be careful.

Think of it this way: don't say or do anything that can potentially harm your business. Even when you think no one is watching, people are, so there isn't very much space for mistakes. Slip-ups are becoming more dangerous by the minute - with today's technology, businesses can fail at the release of one bad picture, video, or statement. The public is becoming much more involved in people's lives but is simultaneously becoming much less forgiving.

Your business is worth more than that - years of time, dedication, energy, and money shouldn't be wasted on a bad decision. On top of that, bad decisions shouldn't even be made. If you're truly passionate about what you and your business stand for, it should be easy to represent that in every part of your life. With each decision you make, you should be thinking about how it could potentially affect your business. For example, each time you make a post to social media, you should be considering what the whole world would think if they saw it - how would that post change people's opinions on you, if at all?

This idea carries over into every aspect of what you do each day. As human beings, we all find ourselves in situations that make us angry, uncomfortable, or sad. We all have our bad moments (I have them *all* the time). The key is not letting those bad moments affect how you feel about yourself and your business - people will certainly challenge you, but you can't let them change you. When something strikes a nerve, take a minute (or even a couple hours) to think about it before responding to it - is it worth flipping out? Probably not.

The thing about being an entrepreneur is, your business is always the most important part of your life. It is the inanimate version of you, and you are the real-life embodiment of all it stands for. You work tirelessly so your business can succeed and acting out during a bad moment is *never* worth giving up all you've worked for. Take a breath, remember how much your business is worth, and respond to situations appropriately. A few minutes of stress is not worth sacrificing a lifetime of success.

# Chapter VI:
# Be Two Steps Ahead of Everyone Else
### Stay ahead of the game.

Entrepreneurship is a race - to the next big idea, to the best execution, to the most fame, and to the biggest fortune. Your competitors are racing against you and trying to beat you there, so you have to be two steps ahead of them at all times. While moderate success can be achieved from unoriginal and redone ideas, the best entrepreneurs are the leaders of the pack - major and lasting success comes from being *the first* to do something great.

Entrepreneurs are natural born leaders - we have a desire to carve our own path, not follow anyone else's. While we can certainly use the distinctive paths carved by other entrepreneurs to help light the way, we have to be innovative, refreshing, and creative trailblazers. In addition to hopping on existing trends that have already proven to be successful, challenge yourself to create a new one. Even if no one understands your idea, you can do amazing things just by being different. Being a leader can be scary, and it will definitely force you to leave your comfort zone at some points. It's important to embrace the discomfort, because it means you're leading the way.

Even if you're not ready to branch off and test your luck with a new trend, you can be innovative in other parts of your business. There are plenty of ways to lead by example - come up with new ways to do things in your everyday life. Advertise in a way that's never been done before, redefine customer service, approach your ideas in a different light, and always continue brainstorming

93

refreshing methods for growing your business. It pays to think ahead of the game.

# Chapter VII:
# Watch for New Opportunities
### Keep your eyes peeled.

The goal is to never stop expanding - your business should always be growing so that you can continue to be successful. However, growth doesn't happen to those who aren't putting in the effort - you always have to be ready for your next move, or else you'll stay stuck in one place. Entrepreneurs are always on the lookout for the next business opportunity because we know there is no time to waste in the business world. It's always moving, and we have to move with it.

You never know when your next business is coming. It could hit you in the face at any moment, and you might not even know it. That's why you have to know how to discover new opportunities - the key is noticing them in ordinary situations. Opportunities exist everywhere, and good entrepreneurs know where to look for them. They often come in the form of people you interact with or problems you face - your own personal experience is usually the best place to search for new ideas. No person or thing in your life is too irrelevant when it comes to discovering new opportunities.

## People

The people in your life, no matter their importance to you, are all opportunities. Everyone has the potential to become something great, whether you can see that now or not - your friend from middle school might just become the CEO of some huge company, and you don't want to miss out on that. Don't get me wrong, you should never use anyone for their success, but it certainly never hurts to maintain strong relationships with people. No one can accomplish everything on their own, and you are going to find that you lack certain skills or resources that you need for your business. The best place to search for assistance is in your own social circle - when you have colleagues and friends in the business world, they are usually willing to help you out, sometimes even for free. Because of this, it's important to do favors for others. When someone asks you for help, you should always be kind and almost always be willing to offer your services - when you show kindness and generosity to others, they usually want to reciprocate it.

## Problems

The little problems you face every day are also opportunities for success. As silly as it sounds, minor inconveniences are the biggest money makers - think about how much money Uber makes simply by providing people with on-time rides. The small blunders you experience throughout the day can lead to some of the best business ideas, so it's important to take note of what tests your patience each day. A great strategy that I typically recommend and actually use myself is keeping a journal where I write down the problems I face and the business ideas I can create from them. For example, writing something like "elevator too slow, need a faster elevator" only takes a second, and is a legit business idea. Taking those few minutes at the end of the day to jot down your thoughts is more beneficial than you'd think. Even if it seems really irrelevant, it might be something that can bring you success in the future.

# COMFORT
## IS THE ENEMY OF SUCCESS.

### BRENDAN COX

# Chapter VIII:
# Stay Hungry
## Don't be complacent.

Good entrepreneurs are never truly satisfied because we know the work is never really done. A huge part of being successful is making sure you're always working to hold onto that success, so it doesn't escape you - an athlete doesn't stop training when they win the championship, they train harder for the next competition. If you're complacent with where you are, your competitors will slowly creep up behind you and pretty soon you'll be last in the race - if you just keep running, you'll never fall behind.

You can't let yourself get comfortable. You always have to feel like what you have right now is not enough, and you have to recognize that you can always create something better. The best entrepreneurs are not satisfied with their businesses- when they reach their goals, they set new ones. The day you feel like you've accomplished enough is the day your success slowly starts to fade, but that day doesn't have to come if you don't let it. I like to look at it like a ladder: when you get to the top, add another rung - and always keep adding rungs.

This is not to say that we entrepreneurs don't deserve some rest and relaxation - it's OK to take a breather after you achieve something big. Everyone should enjoy their big moments, but the key is never becoming too caught up in these moments that you lose sight of your next step. Enjoying the fruits of your labor should only motivate you to do it all over again. Even while you're celebrating a big win, you have to be mindful of continuing your path - entrepreneurs that change the world are entrepreneurs that have always kept moving.

Entrepreneurship is all about staying hungry. It's about learning new things every day, thinking all the time, and constantly working on your next project. I know it sounds exhausting, but true entrepreneurs thrive off of their desire to keep moving. At no point should you ever stop learning, creating, or brainstorming, and at no point should you abandon your enthusiasm or eagerness to try new things. You should always be hungry for further success and growth. **If you're not hungry, you'll starve.**

# Chapter IX:
# Be Open Minded
## *Step out of your comfort zone.*

You cannot be a successful entrepreneur if you're not open to new ideas. Even if you believe strongly in your own vision, you should always be willing to listen to others and accept alternate perspectives. The opinions of other people are often your best sources of advice (and luckily, listening to people talk is usually free). Being an open-minded person is an essential part of succeeding as an entrepreneur.

Taking criticism is always hard. No one ever wants to hear anything negative about themselves or their business. However, you will come across people who have much more experience than you, and they may happen to disagree with your vision. Instead of allowing any criticism to discourage you, take it as a helpful tool for the future - entrepreneurs with extensive experience are our most valuable teachers.

Another part of keeping an open mind in the business world is stepping out of your comfort zone. In order to be successful, you have to be willing to take risks and embark on journeys you may not always be comfortable with. While having stability in your life is a good thing, being in a constant state of comfort is not healthy for growth - everyday, you should challenge yourself to do something that makes you nervous. You can't learn new things unless you try new things.

The good thing about stepping out of your comfort zone is that you can always step back into it - if things start to feel out of control, you can decide to take a breather and try again. You shouldn't ever be so uncomfortable that you begin to feel unhappy because at the end of the day, you are working to please yourself. Take chances that excite *you*. The point of being open-minded is expanding your skill set and experience so you can be the best entrepreneur possible - comfort is nice, but ambition is what takes you to the top.

# Chapter X:
# Think Critically
## *Exercise your mind.*

The best part of being an entrepreneur is being able to see the world in a way that no one else can. While the average person sees problems, an entrepreneur sees money-making solutions. Our worldview is completely different, and it enables us to innovate in ways no one else can comprehend - with our critical thinking skills, we have the ability to change the way things work.

Entrepreneurs analyze situations deeper than anyone else - to put it simply, we think outside the box. Typically, people make assumptions based on what is presented directly to them, which naturally fosters a very limiting view of the world. On the other hand, entrepreneurs take the time to look deeper into what they see and draw extremely valuable conclusions from this information. What we learn from our deeper thinking is what we use as ammunition for our success.

Critical thinking is crucial to understanding the world we live in and understanding the world we live in is crucial to being an entrepreneur. Critical thinkers reflect clearly and logically on their ideas - they are determined to make connections between their knowledge and the unknown. In the business world, this is a useful tool when deciding what step to take next. Identifying, observing, analyzing, and questioning aspects of life and business is what allows an entrepreneur to move forward in their endeavors and be successful in doing so.

The goal of an entrepreneur is ultimately the same as that of a critical thinker - both are determined to continue learning. Like critical thinkers, entrepreneurs can reach whole new levels of success - combining the right mindset with enough drive definitely makes a mark on the world. As an entrepreneur, you have to approach all situations with an open mind so you can come to the best and most accurate conclusion. It's more than just knowledge and facts - it's applying everything you've ever known to everything you're ever going to learn.

We don't just solve problems - we solve problems in the best way possible. And we don't just think - we think critically.

## We're entrepreneurs, after all.

# MY SIX SUCCESSS STRATEGIES

# 1.  The 28 Strategy

Direct message 14 people on Instagram every day and connect with 14 people on LinkedIn every day (with a personalized message). This allows you to connect with 10,000 people every year.

# 2.  The 10 Template Strategy

There are 10 templates every entrepreneur needs in order to make life easier:

- o Private message to potential client
- o Private message to possible connection
- o Email to potential client
- o Linkedin connection message
- o Email to press
- o Automatic inquiry response
- o Thank you note
- o Follow up note
- o Company bio
- o Invoice template

# 3.  The Yes-to-Death Strategy

The customer is always right. Do whatever you can to make them happy, even if you don't want to.

# 4. The $5 Flip Strategy

Take $5 to the nearest dollar store and scope out an easy product to resell - gum, candy, snacks, drinks, even school supplies. Sell them individually for profit, and you've flipped $5 just like that!

# 5. 1095 Problems Strategy

Write down 3 problems you experience daily - whether it's really small or really important. At the end of the year, you'll have 1095 problems you could turn into a business. Little inconveniences have become some of the best business ideas in history.

# 6. Boredom Boost

When you're bored, you're really just being lazy - there is always something you could be doing. If you catch yourself feeling "bored," do little things that will boost your business, even if it's just scrolling through social media and looking for new ideas.

# **Acknowledgements**

I want to thank my family and all those who have supported me throughout my numerous business endeavors. Without your support and constant motivation, none of my successes would have been possible.

I also want to thank my friend and co-writer, Lauren Kamienski, for helping me organize my thoughts in a way that really captures the voice and essence of what I do. I am looking forward to working on many other projects with Lauren and want to express my sincere thanks, as this book wouldn't have been possible without her.

Thanks also go to my dedicated team and interns who work behind the scenes to make everything that I do possible. Without all your hard work and dedication, I wouldn't be where I am today.

Lastly, I want to send my well wishes and good luck to all the entrepreneurs out there, regardless of your age and accomplishments. Keep hustling and working hard to chase your dreams.

Brendan Cox

# Keep Up with my Entrepreneurial Endeavors!

@BrendanACox

Learn more about me:
*BrendanACox.com*

Made in the USA
Monee, IL
03 August 2022